The Sussex Millennium Book

David Arscott

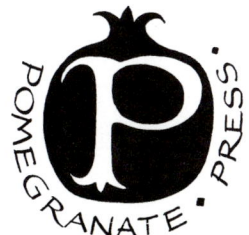

If you've enjoyed *The Sussex Millennium Book*, you're ready for David Arscott's compelling Sussex history, *The Sussex Story*. A guide to the unfolding drama of our Sussex past, it recreates the great and colourful events of local and national history as a series of verbal snapshots focusing on memorable incidents and individuals.

Its special features include:

• a page-by-page scroll of significant dates

• a period-by-period digest of places to visit, complete with map references

• an area-by-area gazetteer of the hundreds of sites featured

Handsomely illustrated, *The Sussex Story* is published by Pomegranate Press and is available from David Arscott's Sussex Book Club at Church Cottage, Westmeston, Hassocks, Sussex BN6 8RH.

The Sussex Book Club brings members details of the latest local publications without obligation to buy. Membership is free.

British Library Cataloguing-in-Publication Data.
A catalogue record for this book is available from the British Library.

ISBN 0-9533493-4-9

Photographic credits (figures refer to centuries): National Remote Sensing Centre Ltd 1, 9, 13; Fishbourne Roman Palace, Sussex Archaeological Society 2; Worthing Museum and Art Gallery 5; Barbican House Museum, Sussex Archaeological Society 6, 8; Dean and Chapter of Ripon Cathedral 7; National Maritime Museum (Armada painting: English School, c. 16th century) 16; Terry Heathcote 18; British Engineerium 19; Evening Argus, Brighton/Simon Dack 20.

Published by Pomegranate Press, Church Cottage, Westmeston, Sussex BN6 8RH
Phone/fax 01273 846743 E-mail: 106461.1316@compuserve.com
Printed by Ghyllprint Ltd, The Ghyll Print Centre, Heathfield, Sussex TN21 8AW

This copy of The Sussex Millennium Book belongs to

_____

*Your
photograph*

signed at the Millennium Moment, midnight December 31, 1999/2000

_____

Millennium Me

*T*his is *your* page - the page on which you establish your own place in the Sussex story.

Use it to personalise your book. You may wish to cover it with photographs, either of you and your friends and family at the Millennium Moment itself or of the people and things that matter most to you. Make sure you caption them, so that future generations will know what they're looking at.

You may, on the other hand, prefer to paste in a sheet (whether handwritten or created on a word processor) which leaves a record of the sort of person you are. It's impossible to know what will fascinate people a hundred years from now, but do give some details of the things that interest you: the 'trivia' of yesteryear is often what appeals to us.

1st Century

The massive ramparts of Iron Age hillforts stand out along the downland crests at the time of Christ's birth – but the Roman legions will soon be on their way.

The Roman historian Strabo tells us that the tribes in southern Britain exported corn, cattle, hides, hunting-dogs and slaves, importing gold, silver and tin from other parts of Britain, olive oil, wine and fabrics from continental Europe.

Their hillforts (like the one at the Trundle, *right*) dominated the downland skyline, but the Romans had no need to test their effectiveness: the local ruler Cogidubnus, long a friend of the empire, welcomed them in.

Vespasian's Second Augusta legion created a garrison at what was to become Chichester to launch an assault on hostile tribes to the west. After being crowned Emperor, Vespasian had it developed as a typical walled Roman town with central crossroads. Today's city is imposed upon that ancient pattern.

43 AD   Roman invasion.

75 AD   Work begins on a sumptuous palace (*next page*) at Fishbourne.

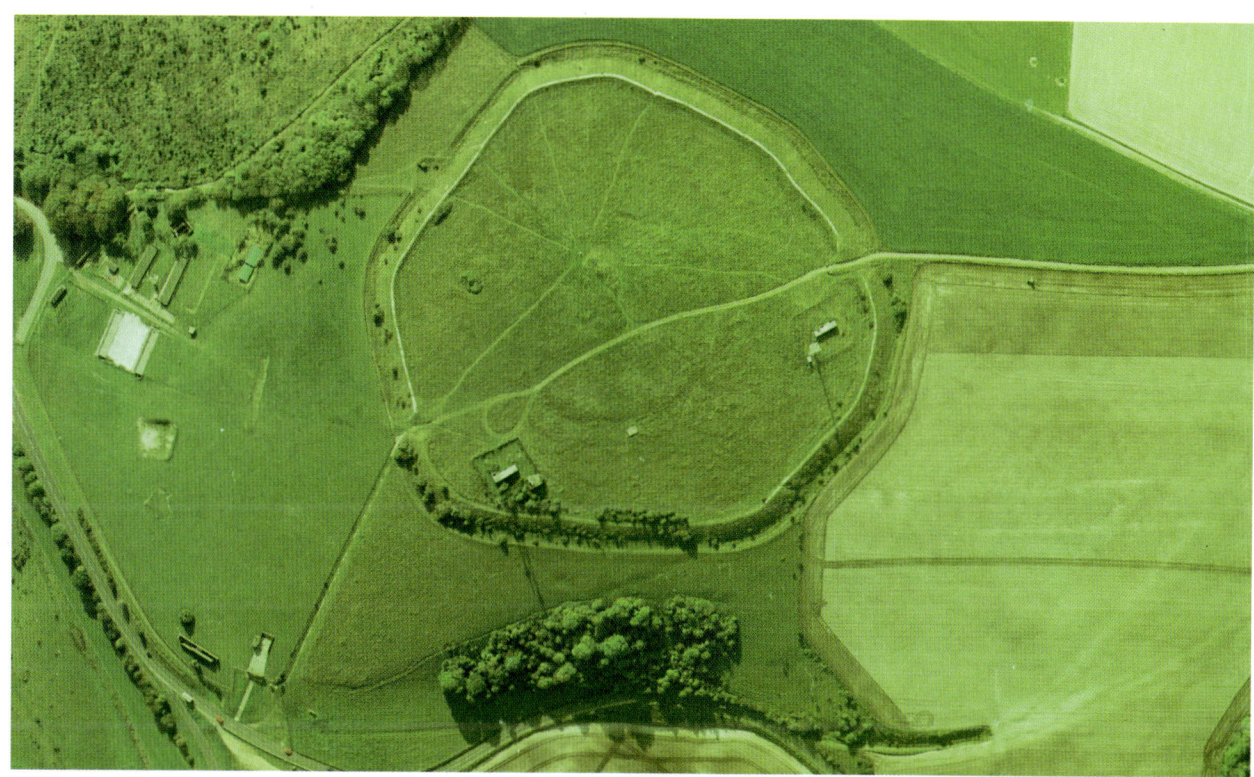

Time travel
IRON AGE HILLFORTS
The Trundle 197 SU 877110; Cissbury Ring 197 TQ 140080; Wolstonbury Hill 198 TQ 284138; Mount Caburn 198 TQ 444089; Hollingbury 198 TQ 322078; Seaford Head 199 TV 495978; Belle Tout 199 TV 560958

THE MINERVA STONE
Set into the wall of the Council House in North Street, Chichester, is a stone whose badly worn Latin inscription dedicates a temple to Neptune and Minerva on the authority of the British chief Cogidubnus, 'rex et legatus Augusti in Britannia'.

The map references throughout *The Sussex Millennium Book* refer to the Ordnance Survey Landranger series. The seven maps covering Sussex are numbers 186-189 and 197-199, most of the county falling within the last three of these.

2nd Century

The Romans are the masters now. They carve three major roads through the Weald from London to the Sussex coast, erect their shrines on the sites of former Celtic temples and build villas in the countryside.

Whoever owned the mighty palace at Fishbourne was a powerful man, which is why it has traditionally been associated with the client king Cogidubnus. Fashioned by foreign craftsmen, it covered 5.6 acres and had all the luxurious trappings of the time, including bath houses, underfloor heating (hypocausts), elaborate mosaics, fine statuary and a large and well-stocked garden.

The palace (*model right*) was at its peak in the early decades of the 2nd century. By this time the Romans were growing vast amounts of corn on the fertile land in the south-west corner of the county, planting vineyards in a climate warmer than today's and extracting iron from their 'bloomeries' in the Weald. Merchandise and the military moved between Sussex and London via three major Roman roads - but many minor routes were created across the countryside, too, servicing local villas and farmsteads.

190 AD First stage of villa built at Bignor.

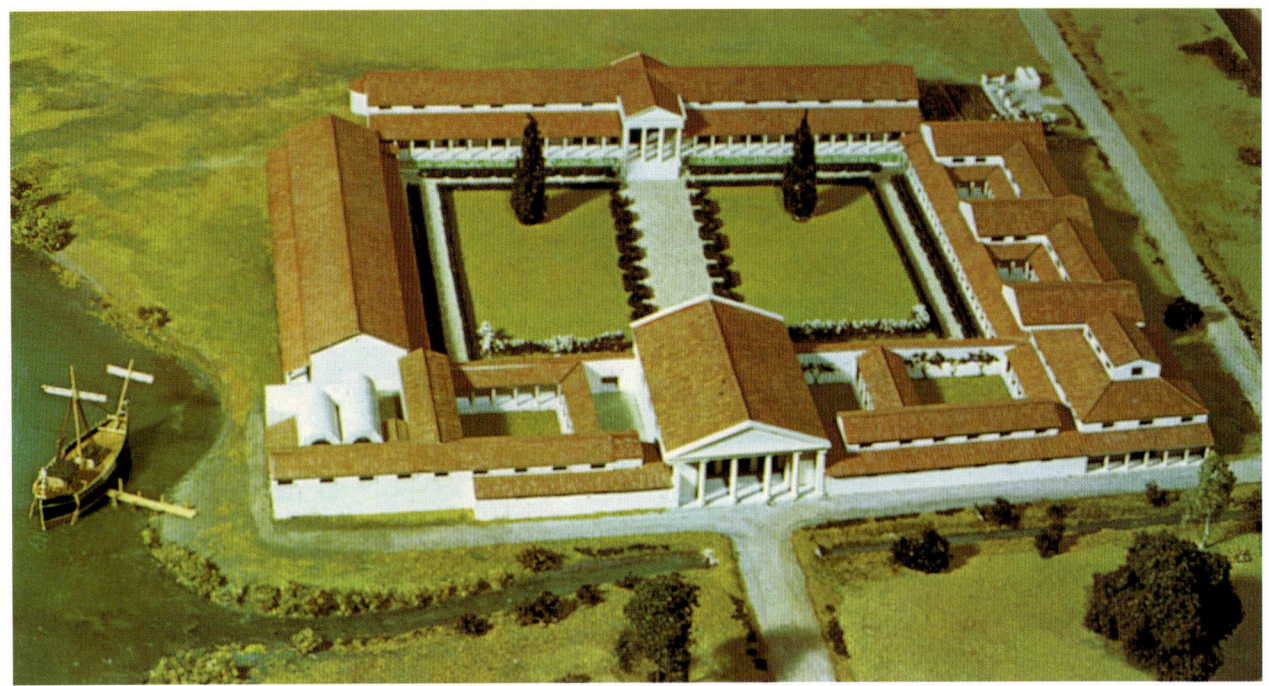

Time travel

FISHBOURNE ROMAN PALACE 197 SU 840052 (Sussex Archaeological Society; telephone 01243 785859)
• Look out for...the magnificent mid-second century 'Cupid on a dolphin' mosaic in the north wing which comprises some 375,000 tesserae and includes what may be the mosaicist's bird signature on one of the borders; the formal garden re-planted to the original plan.
LONDON-LEWES ROMAN ROAD VISIBLE AT Holteye 188 TQ 462387; Camp Hill, Ashdown Forest 188/198 TQ 471290

STANE STREET VISIBLE AT Eartham Wood 197 SU 904105
POSTING STATIONS ON ROMAN ROADS Alfoldean 187 TQ 117330; Iping Marsh 197 SU 844260; Hardham 197 TQ 031174
MAJOR ROMAN IRON-WORKING SITE Beauport Park 199 TQ 795135

3rd Century

This is the high point of 'the Roman peace' - but by the century's end land-hungry Saxon pirates are marauding along the Sussex coast.

Phase by phase improvements to the villa at Bignor, one of the largest in Britain, reflect the growing prosperity of Sussex during the long years of peaceful Roman rule. Bignor lay at the centre of a great farming estate less than half a day's journey on foot from the great market town of Chichester.

During the second half of the century wings and a portico were added to an original four-roomed building, giving it a much more imposing frontage facing Stane Street, a few hundred yards away. Later still it would grow into a 'courtyard villa', with some of the finest Roman mosaics to be seen anywhere, including *(right)* an intricate head of Medusa, writhing with snakes and set within a border of square red tiles and black Kimmeridge shale slabs.

But hard times were just around the corner. Land-hungry Saxons were beginning to test the Roman defences: did they burn down the mighty palace at Fishbourne?

285 AD   Fishbourne destroyed by fire.

Time travel

BIGNOR ROMAN VILLA
197 SU 987147
(telephone 01798 869259)

• **Look out for...the wonderful mosaics, among them the Four Seasons, Ganymede and the Head of Medusa. The north corridor mosaic is the longest on display in Britain.**

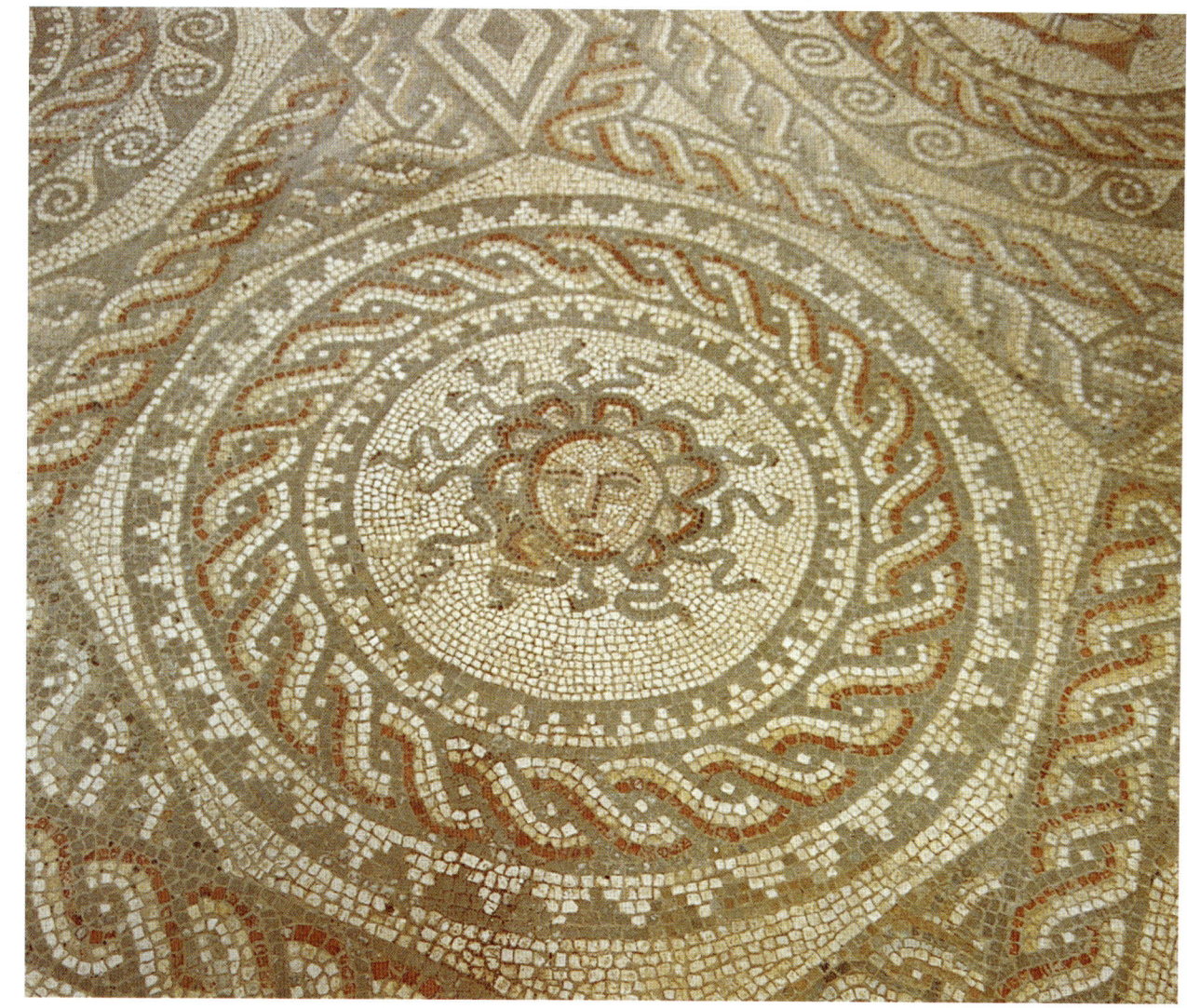

4th Century

As troubles at home increasingly threaten the Roman hold on Britain, the sturdy ramparts of Pevensey Castle are built to keep invaders at bay.

A period of increasing turmoil. Not only were Saxon attacks intensified but, emboldened by weakness at the heart of the Empire, the commander of the British fleet, Carausius, seized control of the island and had himself proclaimed Augustus.

Carausius and his successor Allectus began a series of defences along the so-called Saxon Shore from Norfolk to the Isle of Wight, the last and largest of them being Pevensey Castle. Its massive walls of flint and stone, 12ft thick and washed on three sides by the sea, enclosed an area of almost ten acres, with two solid bastions *(right)* flanking the the main entrance at the southwest. A protective ditch was dug across the isthmus which connected the site to the mainland, and a length of it can still be seen outside the gateway.

Chichester's defences were strengthened at the same time, with the erection of platforms for catapult guns, or ballistae.

340 AD   Pevensey Castle built.

Time travel

PEVENSEY CASTLE
199 TQ 644048
(English Heritage:
        telephone 01323 762604)
• **Look out for...defences from Roman times to the second world war, including the Norman keep and a Tudor cannon.**

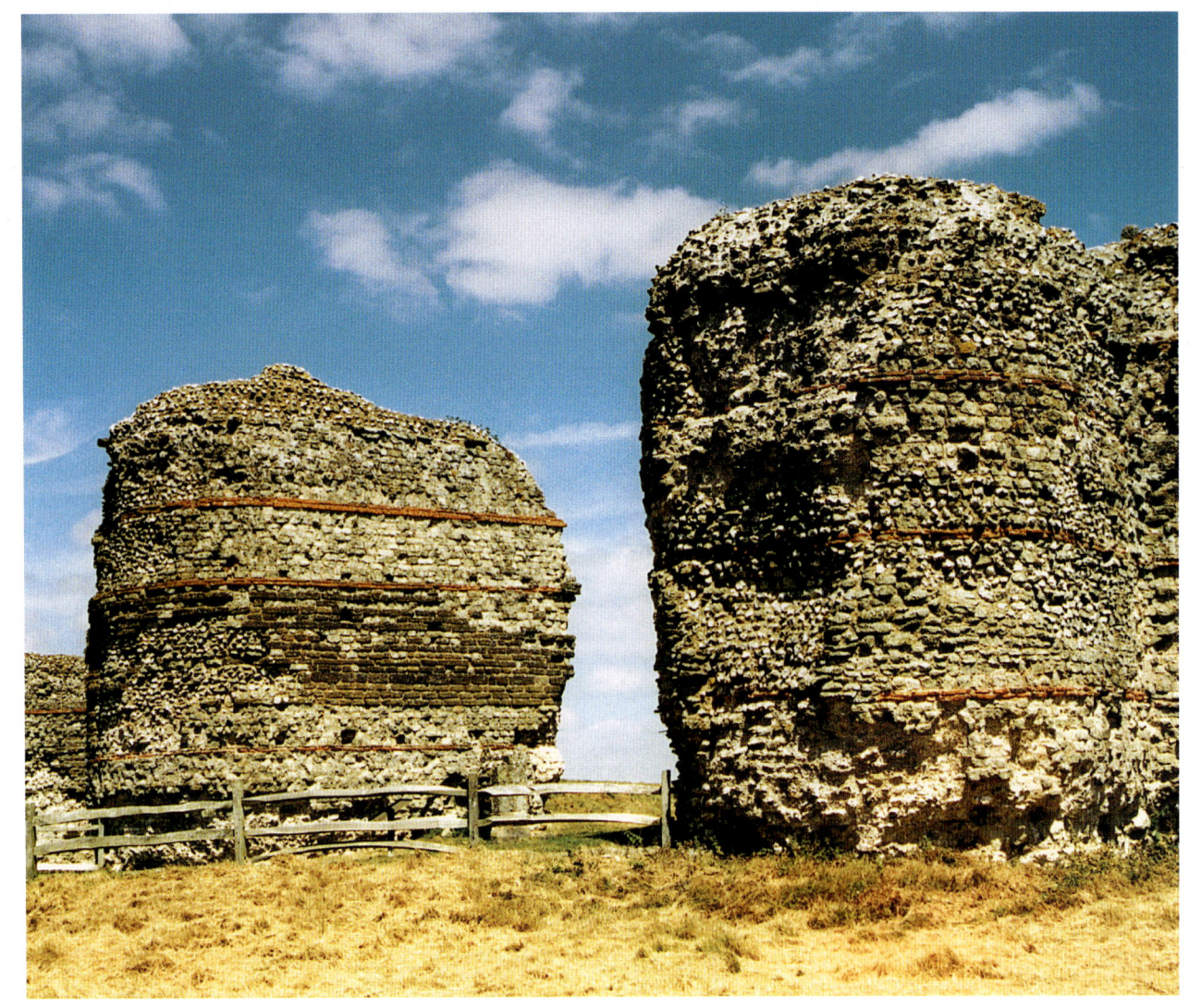

5th Century

The Roman withdrawal leaves the native Celtic Britons at the mercy of Saxon invaders who drive them to the west and rapidly colonise the Sussex landscape.

This was the the time of the legendary King Arthur - the end of the Roman era and the beginning of the Saxon.

With the Empire crumbling and the legions no longer able to defend the island, the hapless Romano-Britons were left to repel the invaders as best they could. The fact that scarcely a place-name exists in Sussex that can be identified as Celtic suggests that the native inhabitants were swiftly suppressed, killed or driven away.

The earliest settlements under the 'bretwalda' (or overlord) Aelle seem to have been between the Ouse and Cuckmere rivers and on Highdown Hill above Worthing, while a separate group known as the Haestingas occupied the area east of Pevensey.

410 AD   Rome withdraws its legions.

477 AD   Arrival of the Saxon leader Aelle.

491 AD   Aelle's troops sack Pevensey.

Time travel   MUSEUMS WITH EARLY SAXON ARTEFACTS
Barbican House, High Street, Lewes (01273 405737); Chichester District Museum, Little London (01243 784683); Worthing Museum, Chapel Road (01903 239999)

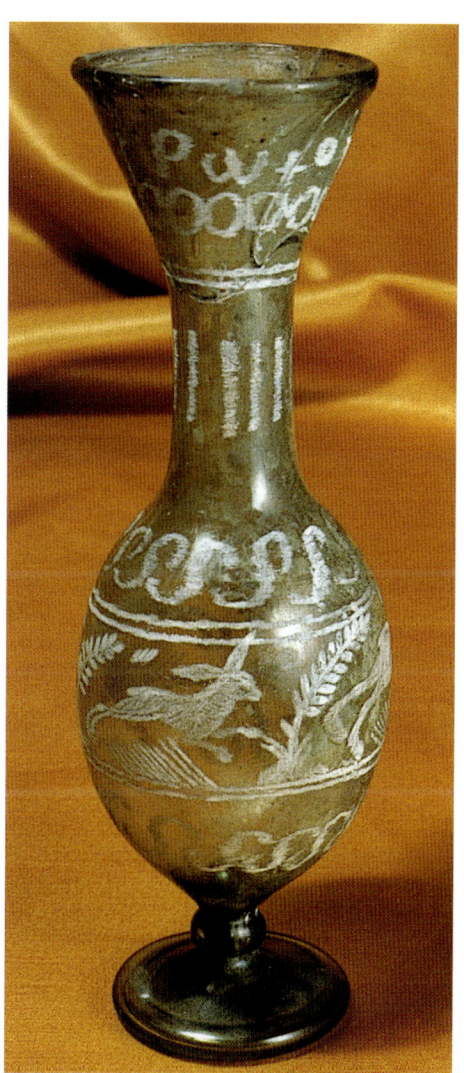

Engraved with a hunting scene of a hound and two hares, this beautiful glass goblet from the Anglo-Saxon cemetery at Highdown Hill, Ferring, is inscribed in Greek: 'Use me and good health to you.' It must have been made in the eastern Mediterranean, and was perhaps looted from a Roman site.

More than 170 graves have been excavated at this hilltop site, revealing a rich array of objects (including quoit brooch style buckles or belt fittings inlaid with silver and bronze) which are now on display in Worthing Museum.

Pagan cemeteries of the period tell us practically everything we know about the 5th century Saxon occupation of Sussex - and that is very little.

6th Century

The Saxons were a rural people (their heavy two-yoke plough would enable them to colonise areas of the Sussex Weald never farmed before), and the Roman towns with their fine buildings seem to have meant little to them. Chichester, deserted by its inhabitants, was allowed to crumble, and the sophisticated villas the invaders found in the countryside were ransacked and burned to the ground.

Exactly where they lived is often a mystery. In Eastbourne, for instance, the sixth century Saxons were burying their dead on Ocklynge Hill and in what is now the St Annes Road area (where Iron Age people had certainly lived before), but the settlements which must have existed close by have yet to be found.

WHAT THE GIANTS LEFT BEHIND

"Cities are visible from afar, the cunning work of giants, the wondrous fortifications in stone which are on this earth."

Through their poetry we discover how later generations of Germanic settlers, accustomed to a humble village life, must have regarded an abandoned city such as Chichester with its high surrounding walls and grand public buildings.

"Wondrous is this wall stone," runs The Ruin, one of the greatest Anglo-Saxon poems, "broken by fate. The castles have decayed; the work of giants is crumbling."

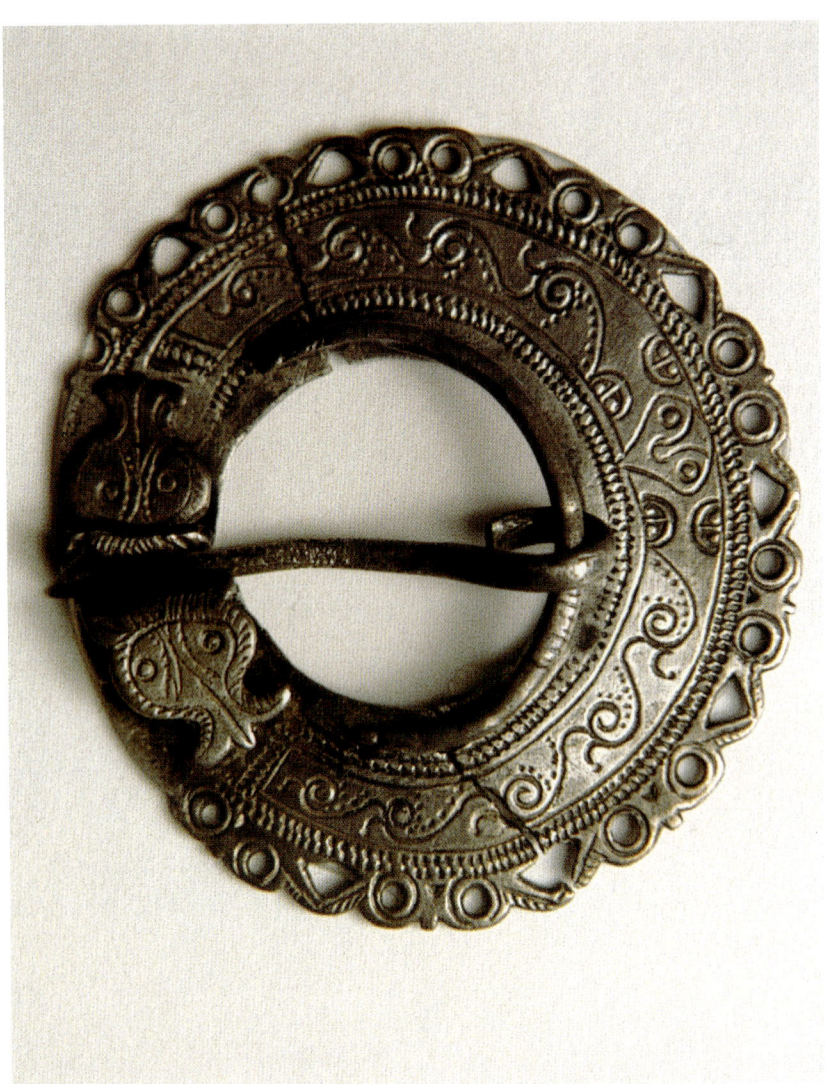

This beautiful silver brooch, unearthed at at the Saxon cemetery at Alfriston and now on view at the Barbican House Museum in Lewes, dates from around the middle of the sixth century.

The site of the village itself isn't known, but the pagan cemetery is one of the largest and richest in the country. Like the one at Highdown, it was first used in the fifth century and has yielded a wealth of fine grave-goods, including glass and other artefacts of Romano-British origin and buckles and belt fittings inlaid with silver and bronze.

7th Century

Wilfrid, Bishop of Ripon, whose career was punctuated by quarrels with the English kings, twice visited Sussex during periods of exile.

On the second occasion, having been granted a large estate at Selsey by King Aethelwealh, he founded a monastery on the peninsula, freed 250 slaves (perhaps descendants of Britons defeated by the Saxons two hundred years before) and baptised the King.

During this century Sussex was an insignificant kingdom, obliged to pay tribute to the powerful rulers of Wessex and Mercia.

666 AD   St Wilfrid's first visit to Sussex.

681 AD   St Wilfrid's second visit: converts the people to Christianity.

BETTER LATE THAN NEVER

Christianity had been established as the official religion of the Roman Empire in 325, but the incoming Saxons were heathens and had no use for the shrines they found. Although the religion made a comeback in neighbouring Kent as early as 597, with the mission of St Augustine to Britain, the people of Sussex seem to have been obstinately slow to follow suit - the kingdom has the distinction of being the very last in England to be Christianised.

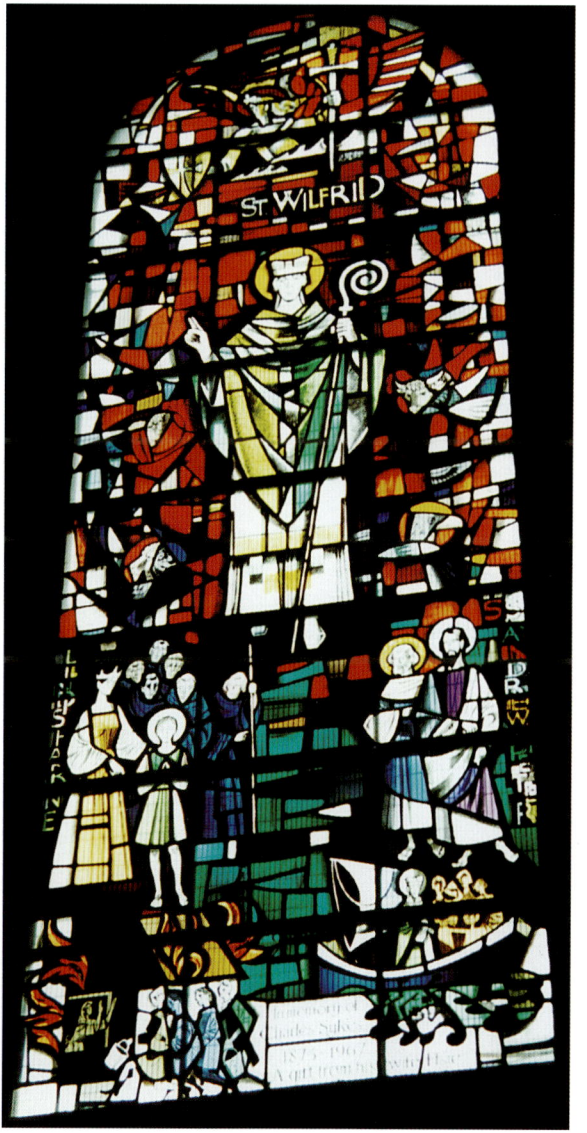

The first chronicler of the English, the Venerable Bede, tells us that St Wilfrid taught the people of Sussex to fish. This rather unlikely claim (did the saint's entourage perhaps introduce more sophisticated tackle from the north?) is repeated in a modern stained glass window *(left)* at Ripon Cathedral: the saint founded the first church on the site in 672, and his original, decidedly claustro-phobic, stone crypt is open to visitors. The window depicts incidents from Wilfrid's life, the Sussex fishing legend appearing at the bottom right.

Bede also relates that at times of drought and famine the lemming-like locals threw themselves from clifftops rather than suffer a lingering death.

8th Century

The first timber churches begin to appear in the Sussex landscape, but the kingdom remains a political backwater, dominated by Mercia under the great King Offa.

Charters of the period reveal the names of the 8th century South Saxon rulers: Nothelm, Watt, Aethelstan, Aethelberht, Osmund, Oswald, Oslac, Aelhwald and Ealdwulf. They proudly styled themselves 'king', but they became increasingly powerless as Offa and his successors in Mercia assumed overlordship of the whole of southern England.

Although our earliest surviving churches date only from the 10th century, many stand on sites which, two hundred years before, had seen the first wooden churches being built in the county.

THE DARK AGES

What used to be called the 'Dark Ages' were given that now unfashionable name because of the little we know about them rather than because of their barbarism.

In fact the spread of Christianity served to make things even more difficult for later historians. In pagan Sussex the dead had been interred along with their precious possessions and household effects - so revealing something of their social habits, their comparative wealth and their trade with other communities.

The new converts, on the other hand, were rarely buried with these grave-goods about them, and therefore left less useful evidence behind.

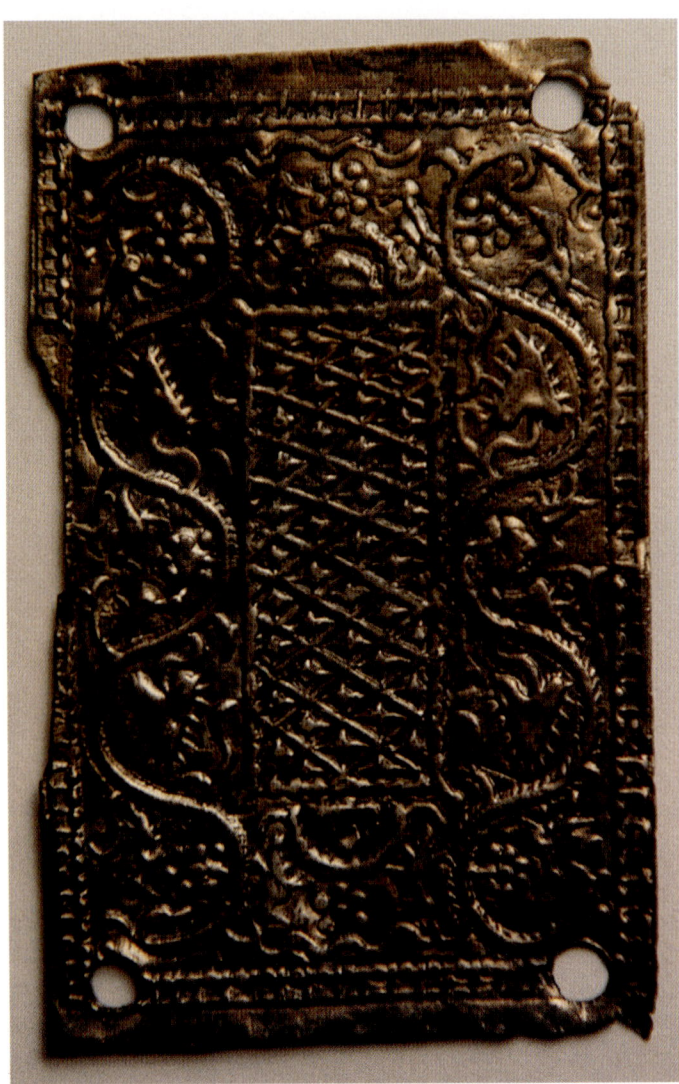

Whoever owned this bronze buckle must surely have treasured it, but for us it remains a Saxon mystery object. It found its way into the Barbican House collection at Lewes long ago, and no record of where it was found has survived.

Clearly designed as an adornment, it may perhaps have been fastened to a chatelaine - an ornamental appendage worn by women at their waist, with short chains attached for keys, pen-knives, scissors and the like. Another possibility is that it was a piece of 'horse furniture', a fore-runner of the horse brasses we know today.

9th Century

A long period of political powerlessness came to a climax in the third decade of this century, when Wessex wrested control from Mercia and Sussex became a mere subordinate shire rather than an independent kingdom.

Worse was to follow. The Vikings, having destroyed Northumbria, East Anglia and Mercia, threatened to overrun Sussex, too - until King Alfred, King of the West Saxons, martialled a stiff English resistance, built a chain of fortresses, including those at Chichester, Burpham *(right)*, Lewes and Hastings, and forced the invaders to retreat into the so-called Danelaw. But sporadic raids were still a constant threat.

878 AD   Alfred's great victory confines the Vikings to the Danelaw.

895 AD   Vikings attack Chichester and are driven off with heavy losses.

> ### A MUCH-USED SAXON PRAYER
> "From the fury of the Norseman, Good Lord deliver us"

Time travel   SAXON BURH AT BURPHAM (northern ramparts by the George & Dragon pub)
197 TQ 039085

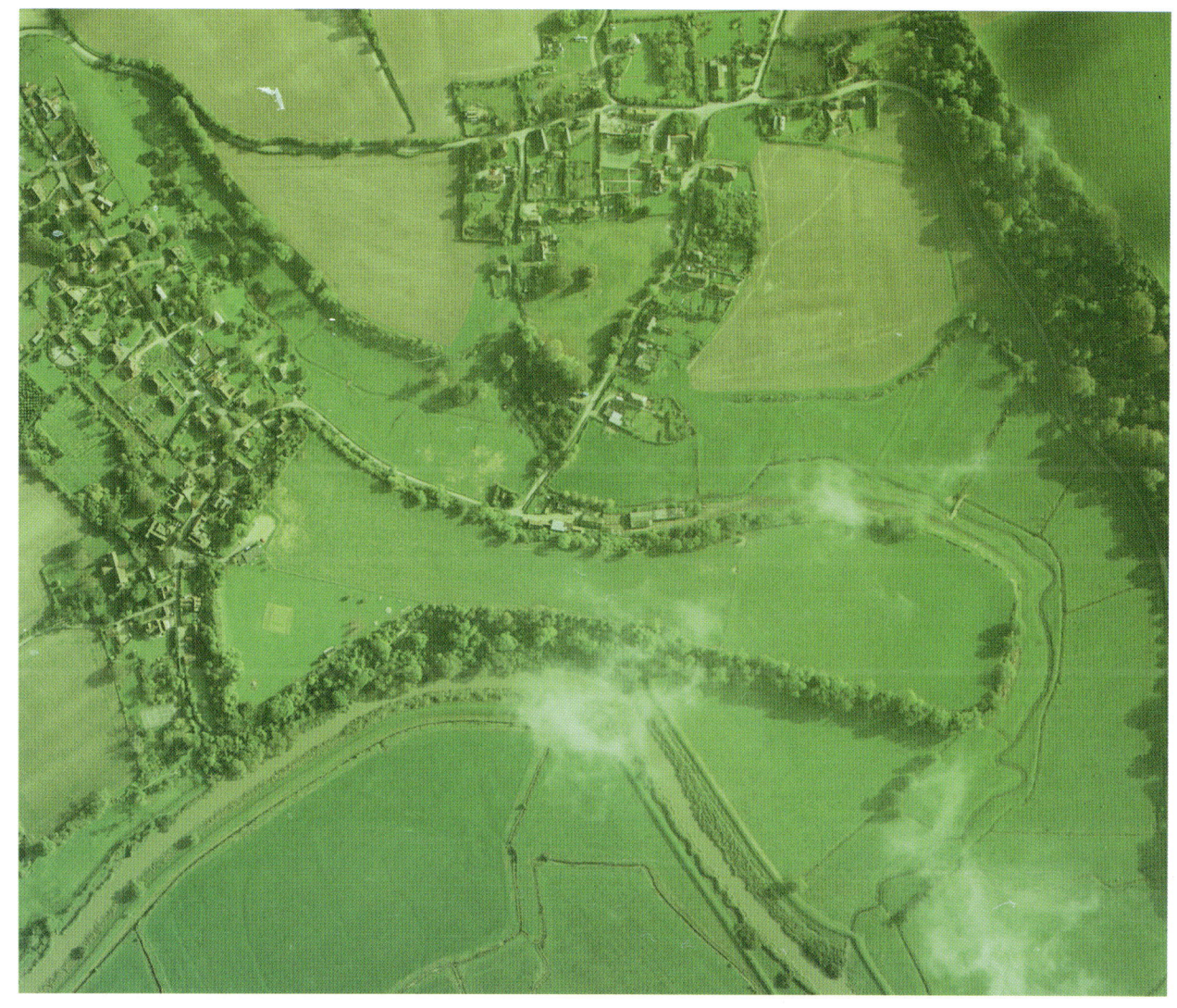

10th Century

A time of recovery and stability is symbolised by the spread of mints and their moneyers across Sussex, but towards the end of the century the Danish terror returns.

With Alfred's successors repossessing the Danelaw and unifying the whole of England under a single king, Sussex at last enjoyed a period of relative prosperity.

Farmers foraged more deeply into the wooded Sussex Weald, moneyers established mints at Chichester, Steyning, Lewes and Hastings and the earliest churches still standing today were built of solid stone - many, no doubt, replacing timber buildings torched by Viking raiders.

A religious revival was led by the great Archbishop of Canterbury St Dunstan, who built a residential palace at his home village of Mayfield. Its chapel has been described as 'one of the most spectacular medieval halls of England'.

By the century's end, however, the Danish invaders had returned.

960 AD St Dunstan becomes Archbishop.

994 AD The *Anglo Saxon Chronicle* reports renewed 'burning, harrying and slaughter' by Danish raiders.

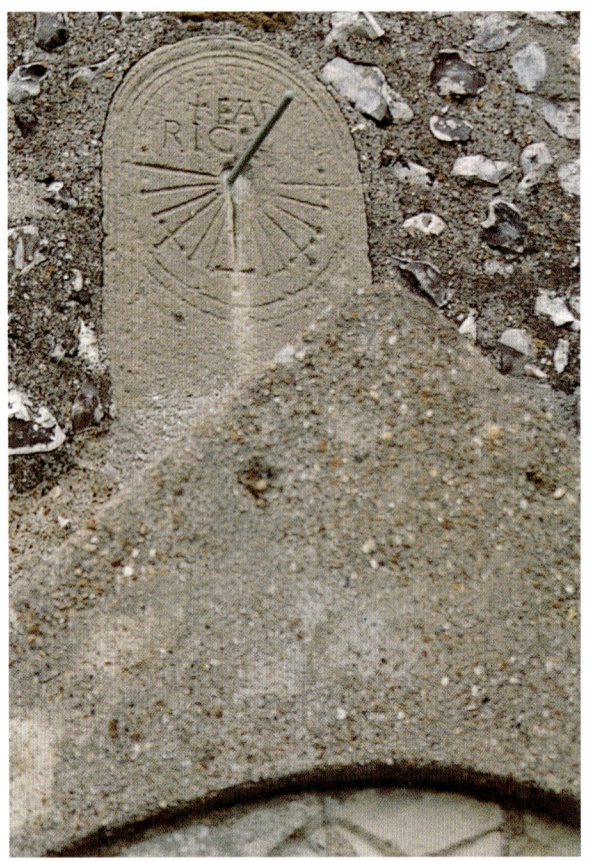

Who was Eadric? The Saxon name appears on a sundial (or mass-dial) above the porch at St Andrew's, Bishopstone, one of the earliest surviving church buildings in Sussex. The cross before his name suggests that he may have been a bishop, but nothing whatsoever is known about him.

The dial, which is set into the original Saxon wall, has thirteen lines. The five longer ones divide the day (6am to 6pm) into its four 'tides', each of these being further sub-divided into three parts.

Dating early church buildings is extremely difficult. The Bishopstone church guide hedges its bets: 'Early 9th century, not later than 10th century, and probably before 950AD'.

Time travel

THE OLD PALACE, MAYFIELD
188/199 TQ 587271
(private, but visits can be
arranged: telephone 01435 873055)

A SELECTION OF SUSSEX CHURCHES THOUGHT TO HAVE
BEEN BUILT BEFORE THE NORMAN CONQUEST
Bishopstone 198 TQ 472010
Bosham 197 SU 804039

Lyminster 197 TQ 022048
Old Shoreham 198 TQ 208060
Sompting 198 TQ 162057
Worth 198 TQ 302363

11th Century

Duke William, landing in Sussex, becomes the last successful invader of England. His barons build great castles to subdue the people, and the Domesday survey itemises everything of value now in Norman hands.

More than six centuries of Saxon rule, punctuated only by the twenty-year reign of the Danish King Canute (1016-1036), came to an end on the battlefield of Senlac six miles north-west of Hastings where William of Normandy defeated King Harold.

Battle Abbey was built on the spot to commemorate the victory, while the Bayeux Tapestry *(right)* was created to tell the story from the Norman point of view. Great castles rose up to defend the main rivers, and the Roman fort at Pevensey was massively extended.

Norman domination was swift. Within ten years the 'Domesday' commissioners had visited every town, village and hamlet in Sussex to assess the people for tax purposes.

1066 (Sept 28) Battle of Stamford Bridge. Harold defeats Harald Hardrada.

1066 (Oct 14) Battle of Hastings. Harold is killed.

1086 Domesday survey.

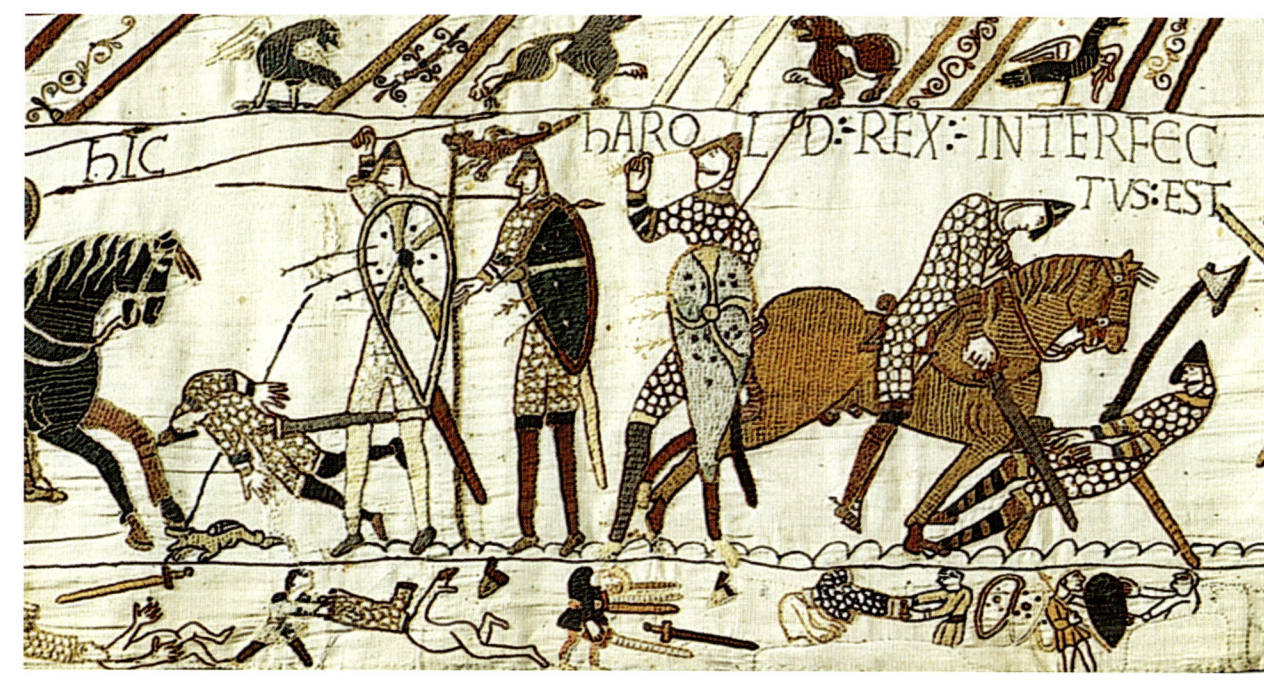

Time travel

BATTLE ABBEY
199 TQ 748157
(English Heritage:
telephone 01424 773792)
• Look out for...the high altar, supposedly at the spot where Harold fell; the vaulted novices' chamber; the site of the battlefield.

MAJOR NORMAN CASTLES
Arundel 197 TQ 018073 (01903 883136)
Lewes 198 TQ 414101
(Sussex Archaeological Society 01273 474379)
Bramber 198 TQ 184107 (a ruin)
Hastings 199 TV 822094 (01424 781112)
Pevensey 199 TQ 644048 (see 4th century)

SITES OF LESSER NORMAN CASTLES
Hartfield 188 TQ 482360
Priory Park, Chichester 197 SU 860048
St Anne's Hill, Midhurst 197 SU 889215
Park Mound, Pulborough 197 TQ 038189
Edburton 198 TQ 237110
Knepp Castle 198 TQ 163209

12th Century

With the Normans in complete control of their new kingdom, religious zeal and a spirit of adventure draw hundreds away to the Holy Land on the Crusades.

At once brutal, adventurous and devout, the Normans were ideally suited to the ambitious, and largely futile, Crusades which attempted to wrest Jerusalem and other holy places from the infidel. The most notable Sussex casualty - killed at Laodicea in 1148 during the Second Crusade - was William de Warenne, grandson of the great baron who had been granted the rape of Lewes by the Conqueror and had begun the castle and the priory there.

At home, churches were being built or extended throughout the county, while at Chichester the cathedral that had been started within ten years of the Conquest (and which had survived a severe fire in 1114), was at last completed.

1184   Chichester Cathedral consecrated.

Time travel

CHICHESTER CATHEDRAL
197 SU 859048
    (telephone 01243 782595)
• Look out for...Two rare 12th century stone panels depicting Christ's entry into Jerusalem and the raising of Lazarus; the Arundel tomb, with effigies of husband and wife holding hands; the glowing stained glass window by Russian artist Marc Chagall; the miniature Graham Sutherland painting 'noli me tangere'.

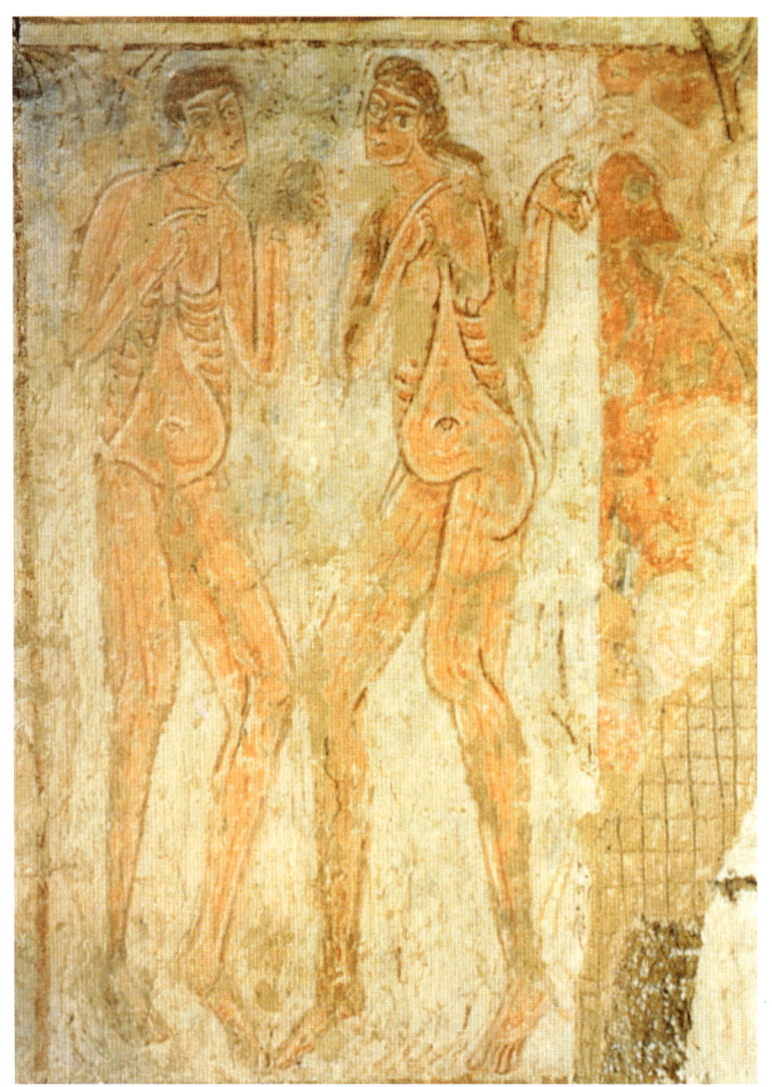

The walls of medieval churches were covered with paintings, colourful representations of Biblical stories for illiterate congregations. Most were destroyed, with so much else, by zealous iconoclasts during the Reformation, but a few have miraculously survived under layers of obliterating limewash.

Wall paintings dating from the 12th century can be seen at Clayton *(198 TQ 299139)*, Coombes *(198 TQ 191081)* and Hardham *(197 TQ 039176)*.

A strong red ochre is the predominant surviving colour, but the vigorous Adam and Eve at Hardham *(left)* demonstrates the quality of the work. The church is remarkable for having its full set of paintings still visible.

13th Century

The ongoing power struggle between the King and his great barons comes to a head at Lewes, where Simon de Montfort defeats Henry III and wins major reforms.

King John's signing of Magna Carta in 1215 is rightly celebrated as a crucial step in the gradual devolution of power from the monarchy to the people, but the concessions forced from Henry III by Simon de Montfort in Sussex fifty years later were no less significant.

Henry's army was routed by the rebel forces at Lewes, with some 2,700 royalist soldiers losing their lives. The King, captured in the Priory, was obliged to sign the so-called Mise of Lewes. Under its terms the new chartered boroughs (thirteen of them in Sussex) were to be represented in Parliament.

Prince Edward, who shared the defeat with his father, left his mark more successfully on the county when, as Edward I, he ordered the rebuilding of the port of Winchelsea (year by year being swallowed by the sea) on the higher ground where it stands today. It's the only English town of the period to be built *(right)* on the continental grid system.

1264 (May 14) Battle of Lewes.

Time travel SITE OF THE BATTLE OF LEWES **Viewpoints in the castle keep (198 TQ 414101) and at Castle Green, above the barbican gate.** WINCHELSEA: **189 TQ 905174** • **Look out for...three medieval gateways; the Court Hall; early tombs in the church.**

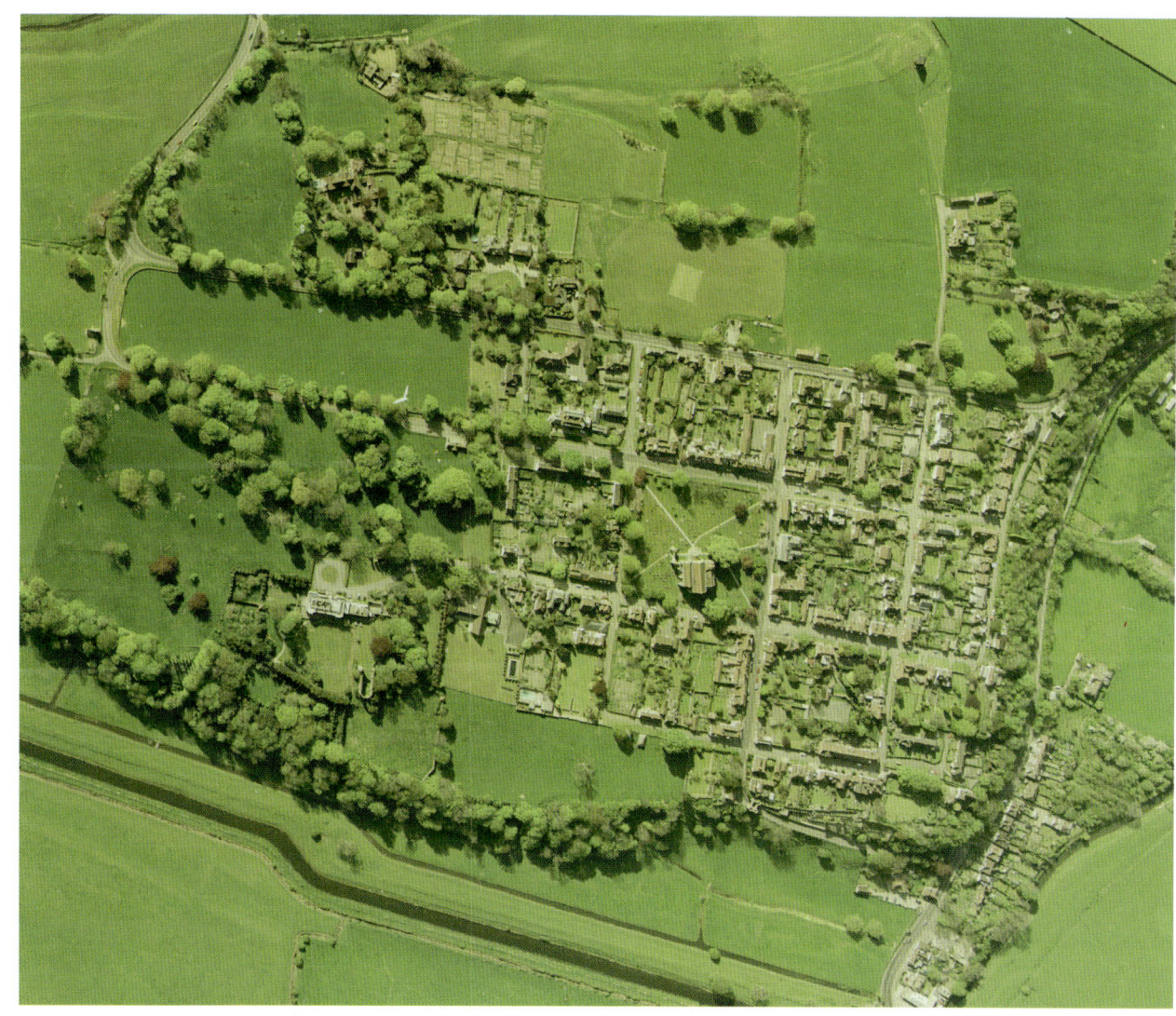

14th Century

A time of misery in Sussex, with the first murderous raids by the French in the Hundred Years' War and the arrival of the devastating Black Death.

Perhaps a third of the Sussex population perished when the Black Death arrived in the spring of 1348. In the aftermath of the terrible plague entire villages disappeared as the survivors, their labour in great demand, built new houses on land rented from the local lord.

As if this were not enough, there were grossly destructive raids on our coastal towns by the French during the Hundred Years War (1337-1453), prompting the building of massive stone walls, as at Bodiam *(right)*.

Not all the defences of the period were erected against foreign invasion, however. The Peasants' Revolt of 1381 was but the most dramatic expression of a general discontent: both the gatehouse at Michelham Priory and the crenellations at Amberley Castle (owned by the Bishop of Chichester) were almost certainly intended to keep local uprisings at bay.

1349   Black Death enters Sussex.

1385   Bodiam Castle crenellated.

Time travel

BODIAM CASTLE
188: TQ 785256
(National Trust:
        telephone 01580 830436)
MICHELHAM PRIORY: 199 TQ 558093
(Sussex Archaeological Society 01323 844224)
AMBERLEY CASTLE: 197 TQ 027132 (private)

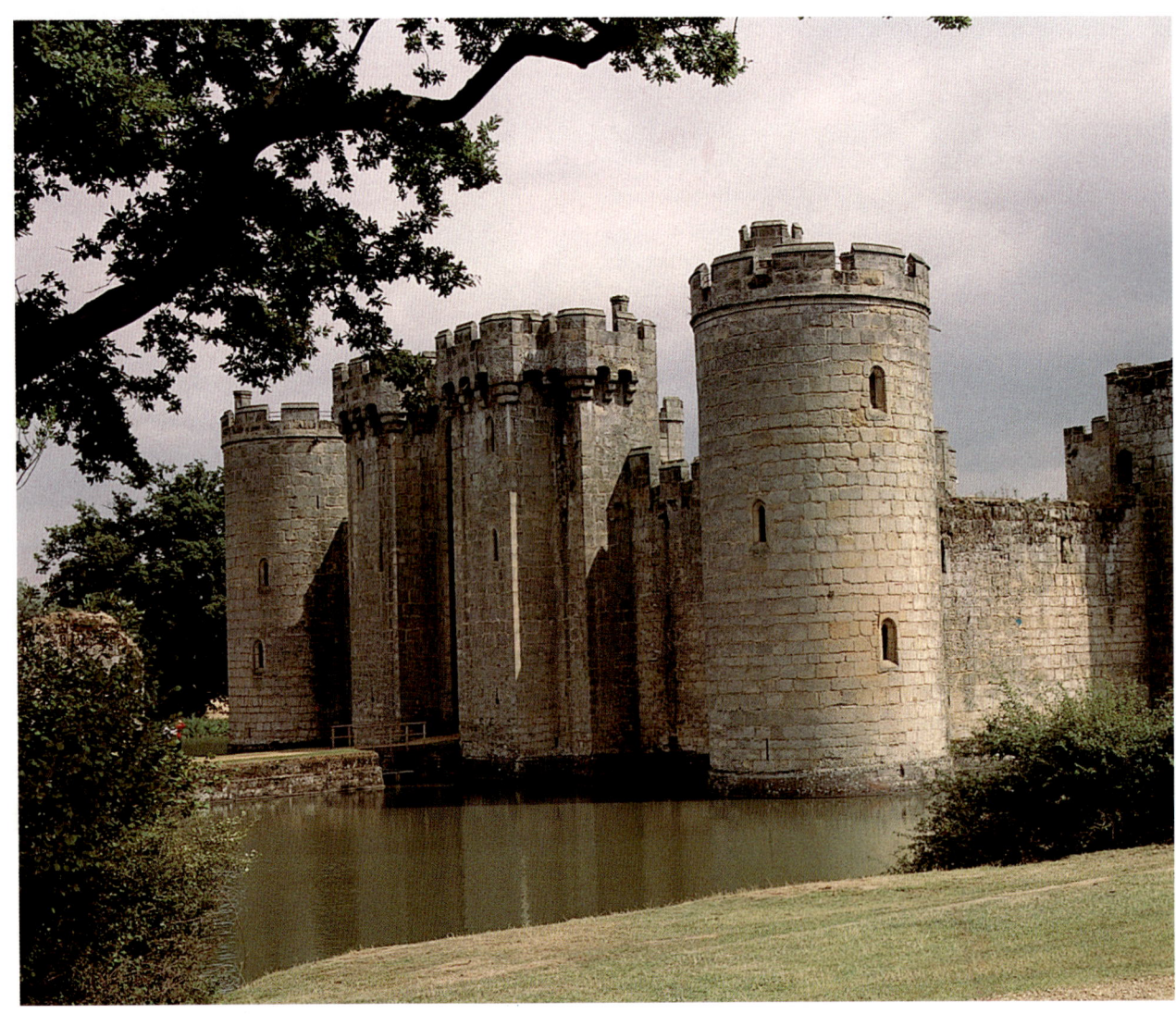

15th Century

Poverty and a sense of injustice, caused in great part by the seemingly endless French wars, at last brought about a rebellion with strong Sussex connections. Thousands flocked to the banner of Jack Cade, whose forces beseiged the Tower of London and decapitated the Lord Treasurer.

Deference to kingship was Cade's undoing, however. He unwisely accepted a general pardon before concessions wrung from the young Henry VI had been ratified: his army evaporating, he was hunted down and killed - possibly at Cade Street near Heathfield, where there's a memorial to him.

Herstmonceux Castle, really a glorified, moated manor house built of Flemish bricks *(right)*, was another fortification built with local unrest in mind.

1440	Herstmonceux Castle crenellated.
1448	Rye and Winchelsea burned by the French.
1450	Jack Cade's Rebellion.

Time travel

HERSTMONCEUX CASTLE
199 TQ 646104
(telephone 01323 833816:
grounds and gardens open to the public)
JACK CADE MEMORIAL
Cade Street 199 TQ 607209 (roadside)

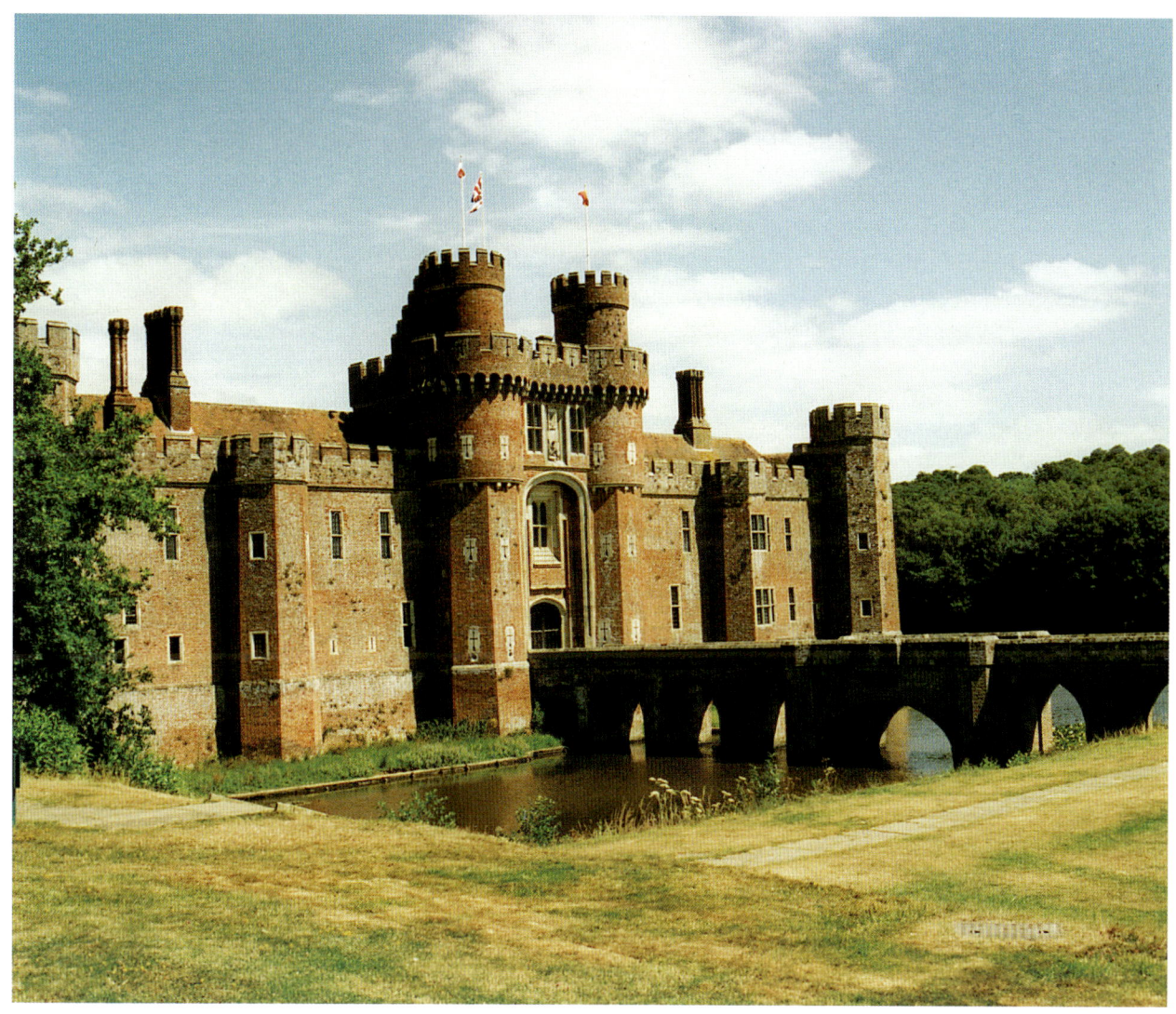

16th Century

Henry VIII's dissolution of the monasteries is followed by a period of religious blood-letting. The Sussex iron industry provides cannon to repel the Spanish Armada.

An era of growing prosperity, with the Wealden blast furnaces producing cannon for the Tudor war machine, was also a time of high drama. The early suppression of Bayham Abbey was a forerunner of Henry VIII's dissolution of the monasteries. The burning of Protestants by Queen Mary (at least twenty seven in Sussex) was followed, in the reign of Elizabeth, by reprisals against Catholics.

Henry had built Camber Castle, but when the Spanish Armada arrived half a century later the Sussex coastline was poorly protected. Mercifully, bad weather and Sir Francis Drake's seamanship combined to save the day.

1525	Bayham Abbey suppressed.
1536-40	Lewes Priory, Battle Abbey and Robertsbridge Abbey destroyed.
1539	Camber Castle built.
1543	First Sussex cannon cast at Buxted.
1555-57	Protestants burned in Sussex.
1588 (July 25)	Armada sighted off Selsey.

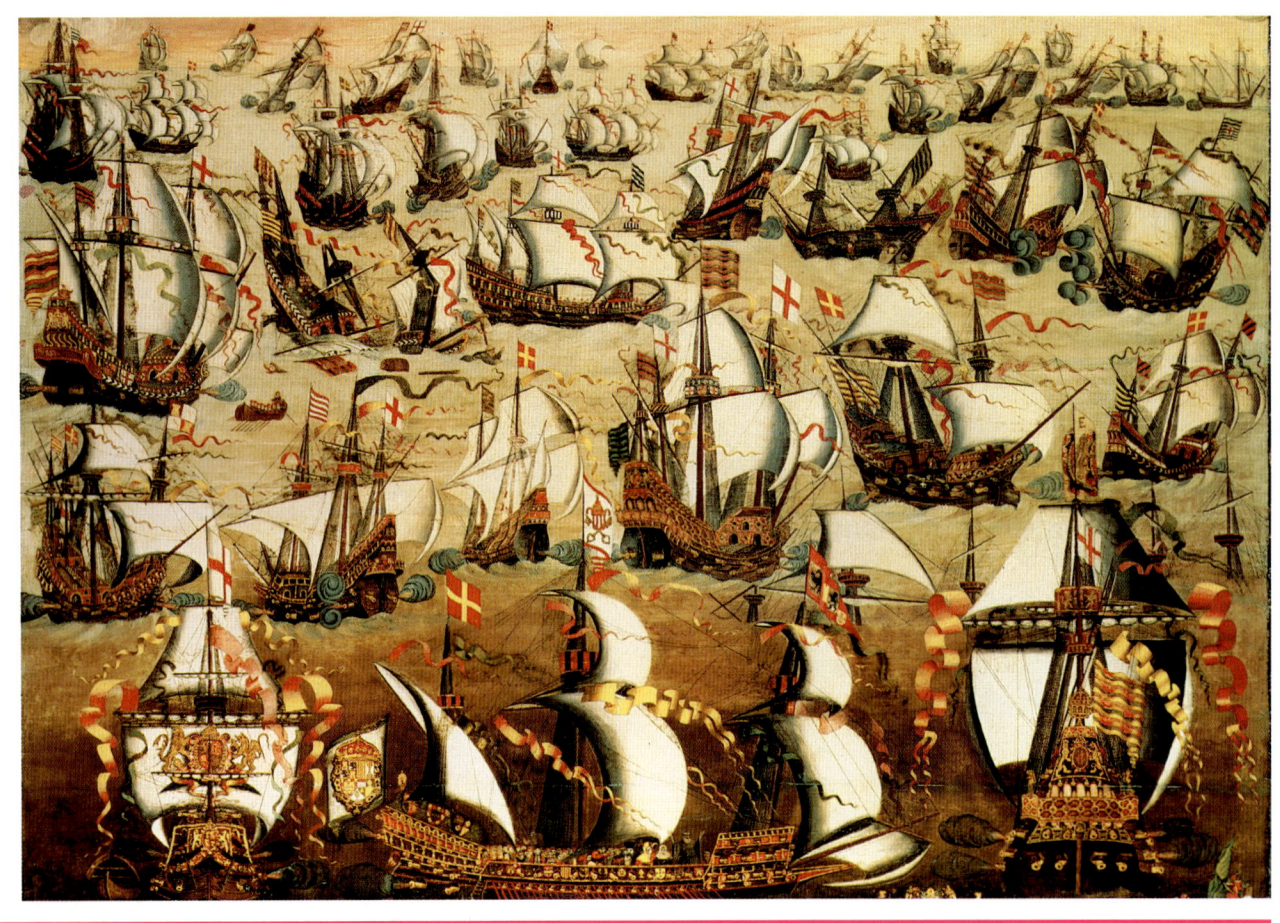

Time travel

BAYHAM ABBEY
188 TQ 651366
(English Heritage;
telephone 01892 890381)

LEWES PRIORY RUINS 198 TQ 414095
BATTLE ABBEY 199 TQ 750157 (see 11th century)
CAMBER CASTLE 189 TQ 922185
(English Heritage; not open to the public)

WHERE TO SEE SUSSEX CANNON
Pevensey Castle: 199 TQ 644048
• Look out for...ER initials and a Tudor rose.
Mayfield (High Street) 188/199 TQ 587270

17th Century

A brutal Civil War divides families and friends. After the Battle of Worcester the future Charles II flees in disguise through Sussex and escapes to France.

A new and confident landed gentry, busy building grand houses on estates formerly owned by the aristocracy, was to find its rural idyll rudely interrupted by civil war.

Although the Parliamentarians controlled the county, capturing Arundel Castle after a seige, they were unable to prevent the 'Great Escape' of Prince Charles - carried to safety from Brighton by Captain Nicholas Tettersell, whose tombstone records the feat in proud verse - and the monarchy was eventually restored.

Parliament reasserted itself a generation later by giving the Protestant William of Orange the crown. At this crucial moment the French attempted an invasion. In a great battle off Beachy Head they inflicted severe damage on the English fleet: the wreck of the warship *Anne* can still be seen off Pett Level at very low tides.

1644	Roundheads take Arundel Castle.
1651	The Great Escape.
1690	The Battle of Beachy Head.

Time travel

ARUNDEL CASTLE
197 TQ 018073
(telephone 01903 883136)
NICHOLAS TETTERSELL'S TOMB
St Nicholas' church, Brighton 198 TQ 307045
WRECK OF THE ANNE OFF PETT LEVEL
189/199 TQ 900140

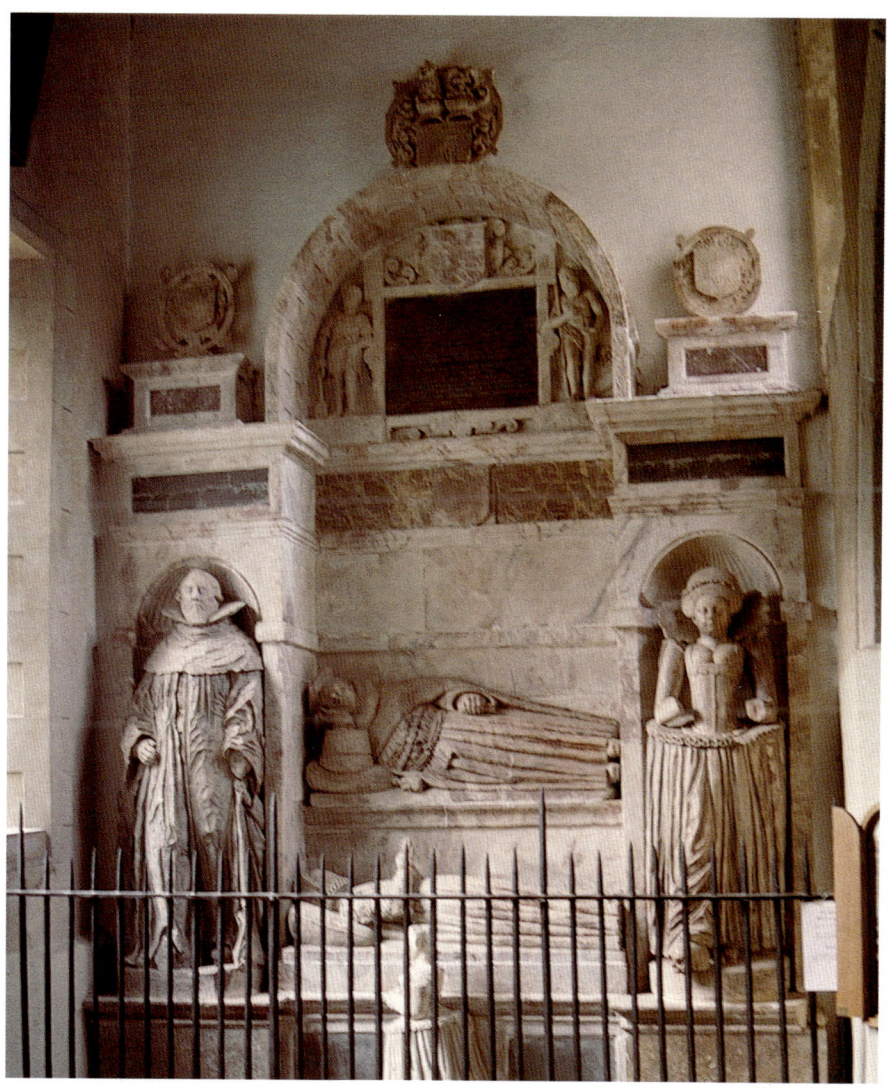

The 16th and 17th centuries saw the rise of 'the new men' - landed gentry, many of whom had profited from the dispersal of monastic lands in the wake of the Dissolution and who wanted the world to know about their new-found prosperity.

The magnificent alabaster monument *(left)* to Sir John Jefferay at Chiddingly church (199 TQ 544142) was erected in 1612. Sir John, Chief Baron of Exchequer under Elizabeth I, is seen in legal robes, reclining on his elbow above the recumbent form of his second wife, Dame Alice.

18th Century

A century which sees the spread of turnpike roads, the birth of seaside resorts and the viciousness of smuggling gangs closes with a new French war.

A series of increasingly severe Smuggling Acts is a monument to this rampant illegal activity (six 'free traders' were hanged in Chichester in 1749), but the period is perhaps best characterised by its elegance.

The wealthy, drawn by Dr Richard Russell's book on the sea water cure, took the new turnpike roads down to Brighton, where the ladies would be 'dipped' by the redoubtable Martha Gunn. In the countryside, the owners of large estates such as Petworth *(right)* had their grounds romantically landscaped by Lancelot 'Capability' Brown.

Revolution was in the air, however (Thomas Paine, who began his writing career in Lewes, inspired both the American and the French Revolutions) and by the end of the century we were at war with Napoleon.

1750	Publication of Dr Russell's book.
1783	First visit to Brighton by George, Prince of Wales.

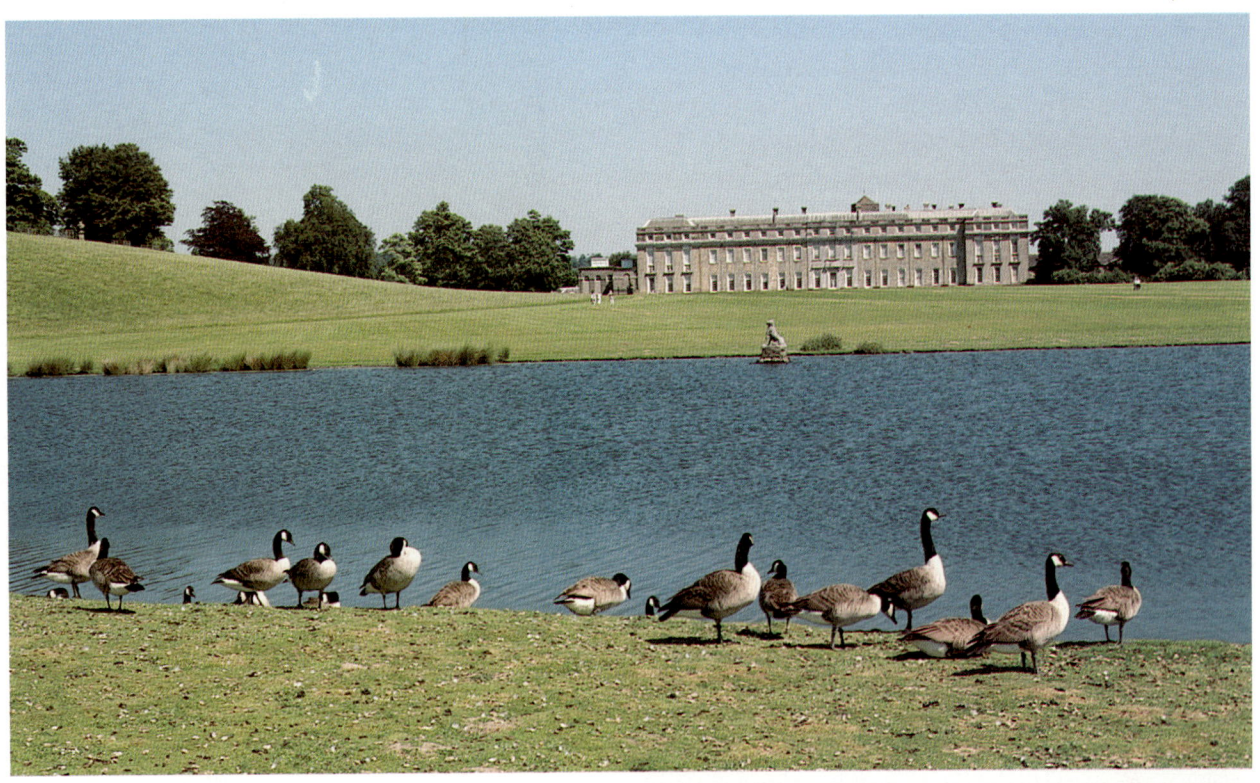

Time travel

GARDENS DESIGNED BY CAPABILITY BROWN
Petworth House and Park
197 SU 976219
(National Trust: telephone 01798 42207)
Sheffield Park Garden 198 TQ 413242
(National Trust: telephone 01825 790231)

MEMORIAL TO HANGED SMUGGLERS
Broyle Road, Chichester   197 SU 860061
MARTHA GUNN'S GRAVESTONE IN BRIGHTON
St Nicholas churchyard 198 TQ 307045
THOMAS PAINE CONNECTIONS
Bull House, Lewes 198 TQ 412100 (private)
White Hart Hotel, Lewes 198 TQ 415101

PUNNING MILESTONES

Look out on the A22 and the A26 between Uckfield and Lewes for a unique milestone design from the turnpike era - a punning bow above four bells. Yes, the distances shown are from Bow Bells in London!

19th Century

The coming of the railway marks the beginning of the modern age. The Victorians introduce widespread public health and education measures to Sussex.

This century of great change began with the erection of coastal defences against Napoleon (among them the Redoubt fortress at Eastbourne and a chain of martello towers), witnessed the bold extravagances of the Prince Regent, later George IV (perhaps the greatest being his oriental Royal Pavilion) and ended on a note of high Victorian seriousness.

If the Georgians left us their elegant architecture, the Victorians introduced public works - sewers, pumping stations, schools and hospitals - some of which are still with us today.

They also brought us the railway network, transforming both the landscape and the local economy for ever.

1822.   Royal Pavilion completed.

1841   London-Brighton railway opened.

1888   County Councils formed.

Time travel

THE REDOUBT, EASTBOURNE
199 TV 623997
(telephone 01323 410300)
THE ROYAL PAVILION, BRIGHTON
198 TQ 313042 (telephone 01273 603005)
• Look out for...the sumptuous Banqueting Room with its dragon chandelier...the magical crimson and gold Music Room...the Great Kitchen, just as it was in Prinnie's day.

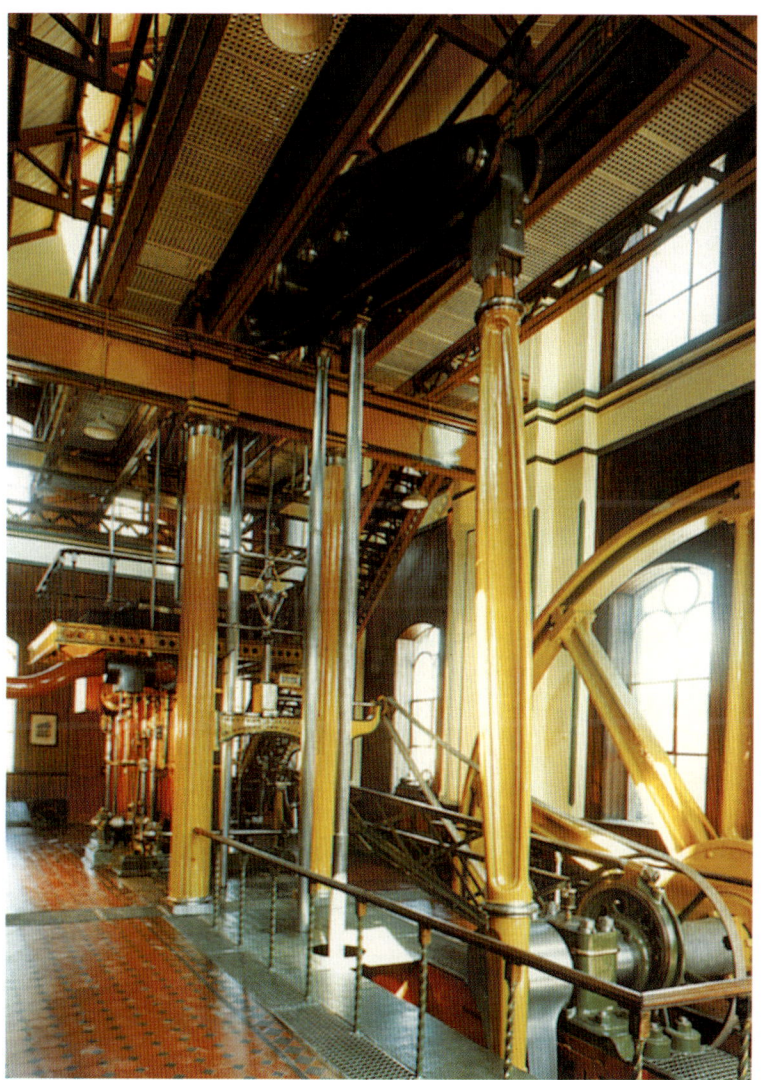

This massive, yet whisperingly quiet, Eastons & Anderson Woolf Compound beam engine of 1875 takes pride of place in the exhibition hall of the British Engineerium in Nevill Road, Hove (198 TQ 286066; telephone 01273 559583).

The Engineerium, a hymn to mechanical ingeniousness, was originally the Goldstone Pumping Station. Its engines raised water from wells 165ft deep in the chalk to supply the fast-growing towns of Brighton and Hove.

Efficient waste disposal was another Victorian innovation. So substantial were the Brighton sewers, begun in 1871, that they are still in use today - and public tours are arranged each year during the Brighton Festival.

20th Century

A turbulent century marked by great scientific advances and the horrors of war ends with hopes of an Irish peace.

We are too close to recent events to know how history will judge them, but the bombing of the Grand Hotel in Brighton - an attempt to kill the Prime Minister and her cabinet - serves as a fitting emblem of a wretchedly blood century. The technological advances which brought unimagined benefits to the ordinary man and woman also bestowed an ability to wreak destruction on a scale never known before.

The people of Sussex suffered time and again: many thousands of young men never returned from the first world war (1914-18); many more were lost and our coastal towns were heavily bombarded during the second (1939-45); and the murderous factional feudings of the Irish left behind a trail of bloodshed in the county.

With memories of IRA atrocities still fresh in the memory (the bombing of the Grand in 1984, the assassination of the MP for Eastbourne, Ian Gow, in 1990), the century nevertheless ended with fragile, despairing hopes of a solution to the Irish problem.

As for havoc with natural causes, nobody who lived through it will ever forget the so-called 'hurricane' which swept through Sussex in the early hours of October 16, 1987. During the most violent storm for almost three hundred years, with winds of more than a hundred miles and hour and barometric pressure falling to the lowest level ever recorded, five people lost their lives and some five million trees were uprooted.

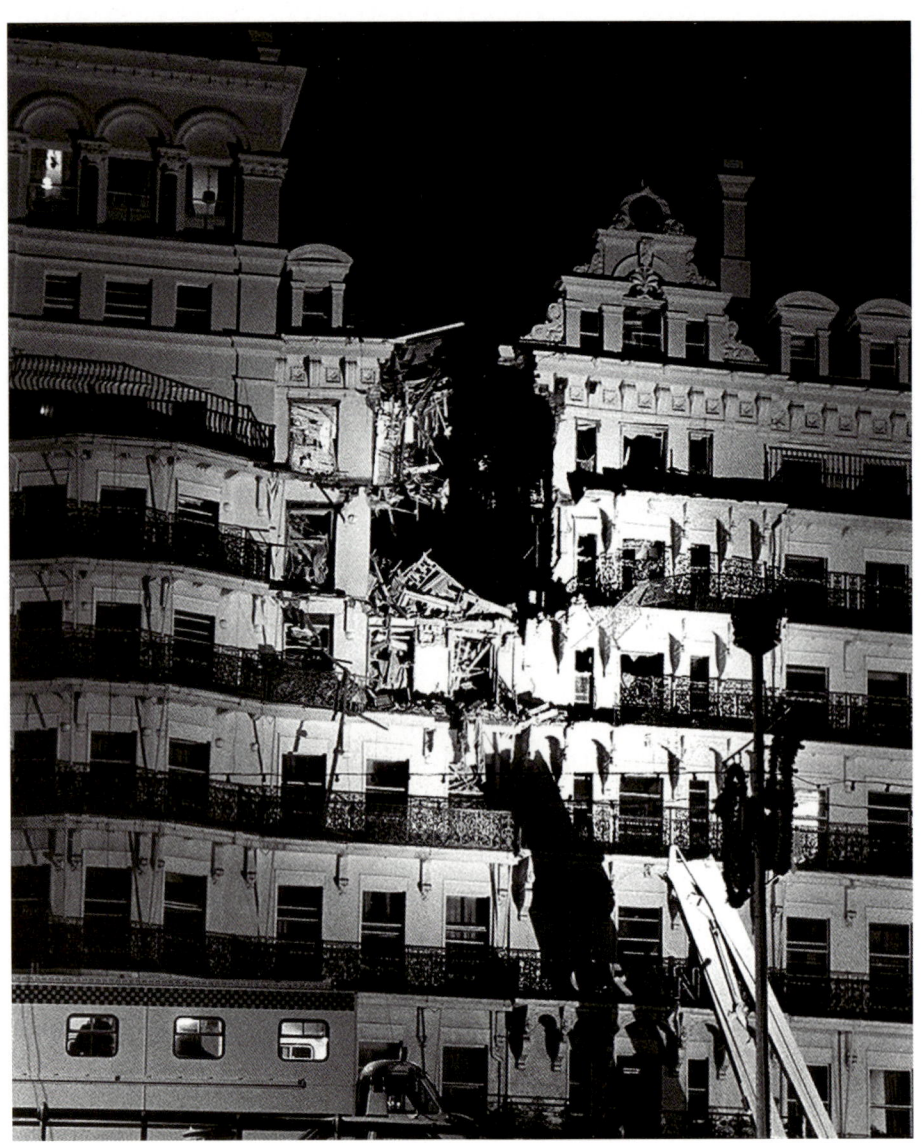

The wreckage of the Grand Hotel at Brighton in the early darkness of October 12, 1984.

Will we learn to be more tolerant, less violent, in the third millennium?